# Table of Contents

# The Inevitability of Action

**Learning: Our minds are always active, even when we're still.**

Ravi wanted to sit still and meditate, but his mind was full of ideas! He imagined himself running, drawing, and even playing the piano. No matter how still he sat, his thoughts kept moving. He laughed, realizing that action is everywhere, even in our minds!

**Action: Try a new activity this week, like drawing or dancing, to channel your energy positively.**

# Intrinsic Motivation vs. External Rewards

**Learning: Enjoying an activity itself brings more happiness than doing it just for rewards.**

Neha and Rahul ran a race. Neha felt free, enjoying the wind on her face. Rahul carried a heavy trophy on his back, struggling to move. Neha finished first and laughed, 'Running is fun when you're not weighed down by rewards!'

**Action: Find something you love to do just for fun, without expecting any rewards.**

# Flow State

**Learning: Being fully immersed in what you love makes time fly and brings joy.**

Aisha loved painting. She lost track of time as her brush **danced** on the canvas. The colors swirled, and soon, her painting became a magical world! She didn't worry about how it **looked**-she was just enjoying the **moment**.

**Action: Engage in an activity you love and notice how time flies when you're fully immersed.**

# Finding Your Purpose: Discovering Your Talents

**Learning: Everyone has unique talents that can bring joy to themselves and others.**

Sam loved tinkering with gadgets. One day, he fixed his friend's broken toy, making them both very happy. He realized his talent for fixing things could bring joy to others.

**Action: Explore different hobbies to discover what you enjoy and are good at.**

# Nurturing Growth: Watering the Plant

**Learning: Small efforts done consistently can lead to great results over time.**

Aarya watered a small plant daily. She never checked if it was growing, just kept caring for it. One day, she turned around and saw a tall tree full of flowers and birds! She smiled, realizing that patience and care create **beautiful** things.

**Action: Take care of something daily-be it a plant, a habit, or a skill-and watch it grow over time.**

# Selfless Service (Seva)

**Learning: Helping others not only benefits them but also brings happiness to us.**

Arya walked into a dark cave, lighting candles to help others see. With every candle she shared, the cave **became** brighter. Soon, she **real**ized she was no longer in the dark **herself!** Helping others had brought light to her own path too.

**Action: Do something kind for someone without expecting anything in return.**

# Action as Sacrifice (Yajna)

**Learning: Offering our work selflessly can nourish and uplift others.**

Rohan loved baking bread. He happily made loaves for his village, sharing them with everyone. Little did he know, each loaf carried a little warmth and love. The villagers felt happy and nourished, and Rohan felt joy in giving.

**Action: Offer your time or skills to help your community.**

# Performing Duty as a Higher Purpose (Svadharma)

**Learning: Every task, no matter how small, contributes to a greater purpose.**

Ramu was tired of stacking bricks all day. 'What's the point of this?' he sighed. One day, he stepped back and gasped-he had built a beautiful temple! He realized his small actions were part of something big.

**Action: Do your daily tasks with care, knowing they contribute to a larger purpose.**

# Detachment from Results

**Learning: Focusing on our efforts rather than the outcomes leads to peace.**

Anil planted seeds in his field with a smile. Some grew tall, some didn't, but he didn't mind. 'My job is to plant, not to worry,' he said. He trusted nature to do the rest, enjoying his work no matter what.

**Action: Focus on doing your best without worrying about the outcome.**

# Neuroscientific View of Karma Yoga

**Learning: Acts of kindness activate the brain's reward system, making us feel good.**

Maya helped an old man carry his bags. At that moment, tiny lights in her brain lit up! Her kindness made her feel happy and strong. She learned that doing good for others also makes us feel good inside.

**Action: Perform a simple act of kindness and notice how it makes you feel.**

# The Cosmic Cycle of Action and Contribution

**Learning: Giving and receiving create a harmonious and balanced world.**

In a small village, **everyone** helped each other. One planted trees, another picked the fruits, and someone else cooked meals. They **all** gave and **received**, creating a happy, balanced world. Their kindness kept life moving in a big, **beautiful** circle.

**Action: Participate in a community activity to experience the joy of giving and receiving.**

# Knowledge vs. Action  The Balance

**Learning: Knowledge and action must work together.**

Arjun wanted to learn everything about swimming before getting into the water. He read books, watched videos, and memorized techniques. But when he finally stepped into the pool, he panicked. His coach smiled and said, 'You dont need to know everything first. You learn by doing.'

**Action: Try something new this week instead of just reading or thinking about it.**

# False Renunciation vs. True Action

## Learning: Pretending to renounce action while still being attached is hypocrisy.

Raj claimed to be detached from **material** things and gave away his fancy watch. But he constantly checked on who was wearing it and whether they valued it. His friend said, 'If you still worry about it, you havent truly let go.'

## Action: Do a kind act without expecting thanks or recognition.

# Self-Contentment and Work

**Learning: A wise person doesnt need to work but still acts for the good of the world.**

Grandfather Ram had enough savings to retire. But every morning, he still swept the neighborhood park and planted trees. 'Why do you work when you dont have to?' asked a boy. Ram smiled, 'Because it makes the world better.'

**Action: Do a task not because you have to, but because it helps others.**

# Leading by Example

## Learning: Great leaders inspire through their own actions.

A king noticed that his people were careless about cleanliness. Instead of ordering them, he picked up a broom and started cleaning the streets himself. Seeing this, the people felt ashamed and joined him. Soon, the whole kingdom was spotless.

## Action: Lead by exampleshow, dont just tell.

# Why Even Krishna Acts

**Learning: Even the greatest beings act for the welfare of the world.**

A famous artist, Riya, had earned enough money to never work again. Yet she continued painting and donating the profits to charity. When asked why, she said, 'I dont paint for money. I paint because the world needs beauty.'

**Action: Do something meaningful today, even if you dont need to.**

# Those Who Follow vs. Ignore Wisdom

## Learning: Those who follow wisdom prosper; those who ignore it suffer.

Two students, Priya and Anil, received advice from their teacher: 'Always start your homework early.' Priya followed it and had stress-free days. Anil ignored it and struggled every night. One day, he sighed, 'I wish I had listened.'

## Action: Apply one good lesson in your life today.

# The Danger of Uncontrolled Desire

## Learning: Desire and anger lead to destruction.

Manu loved sweets but knew too much sugar was unhealthy. One day, he saw a cake and couldnt resist eating the whole thing. Later, his stomach hurt, and he felt sick. He realized that giving in to desire often leads to suffering.

## Action: Practice self-control. Say no to something unnecessary today.

# Mastering the Mind & Senses

**Learning: Control your mind, and you control your life.**

A sailor told his apprentice, 'The wind will always blow, but if you steer well, youll reach your destination.' The apprentice realized that like the wind, thoughts will always come, but he must guide his mind to stay focused.

**Action: Meditate for 5 minutes today and observe your thoughts without reacting.**

# Appendix: Gita Karma Yoga - Verse to Stories

This appendix provides a verse-by-verse breakdown of Bhagavad Gita Chapter 3 (Karma Yoga) and maps each teaching to the corresponding story in this book.

3.3  3.4: Knowledge vs. Action  Covered in 'Knowledge vs. Action  The Balance'

3.5: The Inevitability of Action  Covered in 'The Inevitability of Action'

3.6  3.7: False Renunciation  Covered in 'False Renunciation vs. True Action'

3.8  3.9: Action vs. Inaction  Covered in 'Nurturing Growth  Watering the Plant'

3.10  3.12: Sacrifice Sustains the World  Covered in 'Action as Sacrifice (Yajna)'

3.13  3.16: The Cosmic Cycle  Covered in 'The Cosmic Cycle of Action and Contribution'

3.17  3.19: Work Without Attachment  Covered in 'Intrinsic Motivation vs. External Rewards', 'Detachment from Results'

3.20  3.21: Leading by Example  Covered in 'Leading by Example'

3.22  3.26: Krishnas Actions  Covered in 'Why Even Krishna Acts'

3.27  3.30: Surrender to the Divine  Covered in 'Flow State'

3.31  3.32: Follow vs. Ignore Wisdom  Covered in 'Those Who Follow vs. Ignore Wisdom'

3.33  3.35: Following Ones Nature  Covered in 'Finding Your Purpose', 'Performing Duty as a Higher Purpose'

3.36  3.39: Desire & Anger  Covered in 'The Danger of Uncontrolled Desire'

3.40  3.43: Controlling the Mind  Covered in 'Mastering the Mind & Senses'

This ensures that all major teachings from Bhagavad Gita Chapter 3 are covered through engaging, modern stories.